A message to you King

Creating healthy habits in your life is key to achieving your goals, becoming successful, obtaining personal growth and healing. This journal will help you find the happiness that you truly deserve and strengthen you mentally to create discipline and awareness to your true self. I am proud of you for making the first step to finding your Happiness.

Erika B

Erika_B_is_she ErikaB.is.she
www.plannedaddiction.com

This Journal Belongs To:

_____

Phone Number:

_____

Email:

_____

www.plannedaddiction.com

"Creating healthy habits will lead you to positive results, continuous unhealthy habits will lead you to a negative ending. "

ERIKA BLANTON (Planned Addiction)

www.plannedaddiction.com

Calendar 2022

January

S	M	T	W	T	F	S
						1
2	3	4	5	6	7	8
9	10	11	12	13	14	15
16	17	18	19	20	21	22
23	24	25	26	27	28	29
30	31					

February

S	M	T	W	T	F	S
		1	2	3	4	5
6	7	8	9	10	11	12
13	14	15	16	17	18	19
20	21	22	23	24	25	26
27	28					

March

S	M	T	W	T	F	S
		1	2	3	4	5
6	7	8	9	10	11	12
13	14	15	16	17	18	19
20	21	22	23	24	25	26
27	28	29	30	31		

April

S	M	T	W	T	F	S
					1	2
3	4	5	6	7	8	9
10	11	12	13	14	15	16
17	18	19	20	21	22	23
24	25	26	27	28	29	30

May

S	M	T	W	T	F	S
1	2	3	4	5	6	7
8	9	10	11	12	13	14
15	16	17	18	19	20	21
22	23	24	25	26	27	28
29	30	31				

June

S	M	T	W	T	F	S
			1	2	3	4
5	6	7	8	9	10	11
12	13	14	15	16	17	18
19	20	21	22	23	24	25
26	27	28	29	30		

July

S	M	T	W	T	F	S
					1	2
3	4	5	6	7	8	9
10	11	12	13	14	15	16
17	18	19	20	21	22	23
24	25	26	27	28	29	30
31						

August

S	M	T	W	T	F	S
	1	2	3	4	5	6
7	8	9	10	11	12	13
14	15	16	17	18	19	20
21	22	23	24	25	26	27
28	29	30	31			

September

S	M	T	W	T	F	S
				1	2	3
4	5	6	7	8	9	10
11	12	13	14	15	16	17
18	19	20	21	22	23	24
25	26	27	28	29	30	

October

S	M	T	W	T	F	S
						1
2	3	4	5	6	7	8
9	10	11	12	13	14	15
16	17	18	19	20	21	22
23	24	25	26	27	28	29
30	31					

November

S	M	T	W	T	F	S
		1	2	3	4	5
6	7	8	9	10	11	12
13	14	15	16	17	18	19
20	21	22	23	24	25	26
27	28	29	30			

December

S	M	T	W	T	F	S
				1	2	3
4	5	6	7	8	9	10
11	12	13	14	15	16	17
18	19	20	21	22	23	24
25	26	27	28	29	30	31

www.plannedaddiction.com

Date:

Today I feel...

3 Things I'm Grateful For

1. _____

2. _____

3. _____

3 Things I Love About Me

1. _____

2. _____

3. _____

I am...

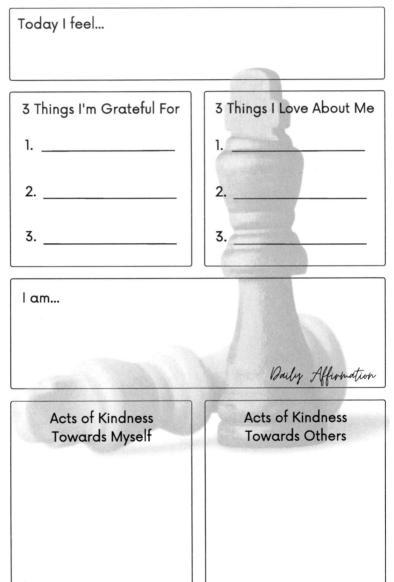

Daily Affirmation

Acts of Kindness
Towards Myself

Acts of Kindness
Towards Others

Date:

Today I feel...

3 Things I'm Grateful For	3 Things I Love About Me
1. _____	1. _____
2. _____	2. _____
3. _____	3. _____

I am...

Daily Affirmation

Acts of Kindness Towards Myself	Acts of Kindness Towards Others

Date:

Today I feel...

3 Things I'm Grateful For

1. _____

2. _____

3. _____

3 Things I Love About Me

1. _____

2. _____

3. _____

I am...

Daily Affirmation

Acts of Kindness
Towards Myself

Acts of Kindness
Towards Others

Date:

Today I feel...

3 Things I'm Grateful For

1. _____

2. _____

3. _____

3 Things I Love About Me

1. _____

2. _____

3. _____

I am...

Daily Affirmation

Acts of Kindness
Towards Myself

Acts of Kindness
Towards Others

Date:

Today I feel...

3 Things I'm Grateful For

1. _____

2. _____

3. _____

3 Things I Love About Me

1. _____

2. _____

3. _____

I am...

Daily Affirmation

Acts of Kindness
Towards Myself

Acts of Kindness
Towards Others

Date:

Today I feel...

3 Things I'm Grateful For

1. _____

2. _____

3. _____

3 Things I Love About Me

1. _____

2. _____

3. _____

I am...

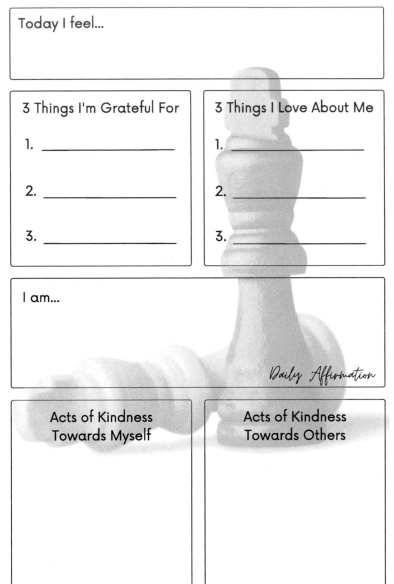

Daily Affirmation

Acts of Kindness Towards Myself

Acts of Kindness Towards Others

Date:

Today I feel...

3 Things I'm Grateful For

1. _____

2. _____

3. _____

3 Things I Love About Me

1. _____

2. _____

3. _____

I am...

Daily Affirmation

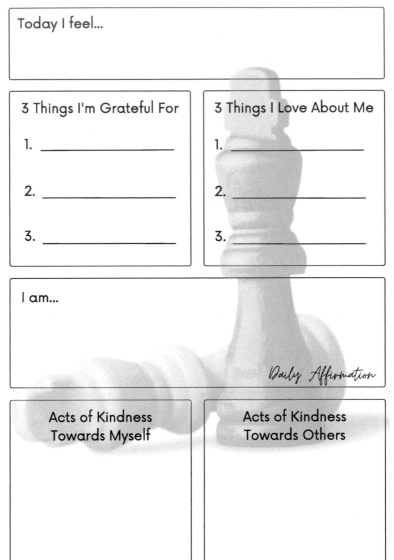

Acts of Kindness
Towards Myself

Acts of Kindness
Towards Others

Date:

Today I feel...

3 Things I'm Grateful For

1. _____

2. _____

3. _____

3 Things I Love About Me

1. _____

2. _____

3. _____

I am...

Daily Affirmation

Acts of Kindness
Towards Myself

Acts of Kindness
Towards Others

Date:

Today I feel...

3 Things I'm Grateful For	3 Things I Love About Me
1. _____	1. _____
2. _____	2. _____
3. _____	3. _____

I am...

Daily Affirmation

Acts of Kindness Towards Myself	Acts of Kindness Towards Others

Date:

Today I feel...

3 Things I'm Grateful For

1. _____

2. _____

3. _____

3 Things I Love About Me

1. _____

2. _____

3. _____

I am...

Daily Affirmation

Acts of Kindness
Towards Myself

Acts of Kindness
Towards Others

Date:

Today I feel...

3 Things I'm Grateful For	3 Things I Love About Me
1. _____	1. _____
2. _____	2. _____
3. _____	3. _____

I am...

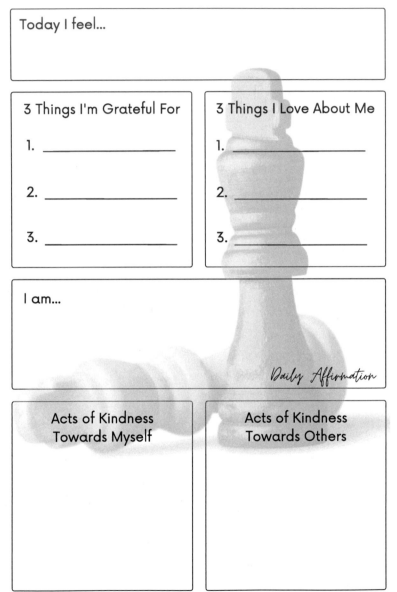

Daily Affirmation

Acts of Kindness Towards Myself	Acts of Kindness Towards Others

Date:

Today I feel...

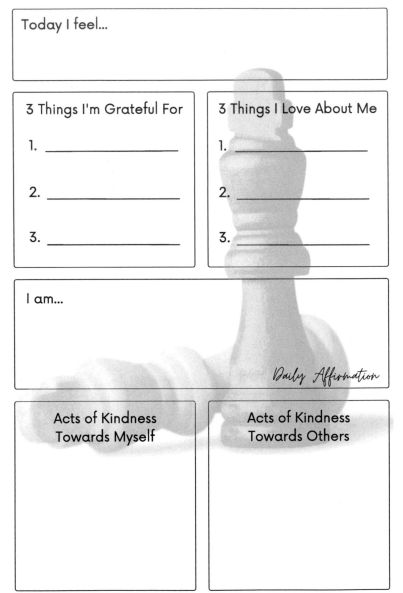

3 Things I'm Grateful For

1. _____

2. _____

3. _____

3 Things I Love About Me

1. _____

2. _____

3. _____

I am...

Daily Affirmation

Acts of Kindness
Towards Myself

Acts of Kindness
Towards Others

Date:

Today I feel...

3 Things I'm Grateful For

1. _____

2. _____

3. _____

3 Things I Love About Me

1. _____

2. _____

3. _____

I am...

Daily Affirmation

Acts of Kindness
Towards Myself

Acts of Kindness
Towards Others

Date:

Today I feel...

3 Things I'm Grateful For	3 Things I Love About Me
1. _____	1. _____
2. _____	2. _____
3. _____	3. _____

I am...

Daily Affirmation

Acts of Kindness Towards Myself	Acts of Kindness Towards Others

Date:

Today I feel...

3 Things I'm Grateful For

1. _____

2. _____

3. _____

3 Things I Love About Me

1. _____

2. _____

3. _____

I am...

Daily Affirmation

Acts of Kindness
Towards Myself

Acts of Kindness
Towards Others

Date:

Today I feel...

3 Things I'm Grateful For	3 Things I Love About Me
1. _____	1. _____
2. _____	2. _____
3. _____	3. _____

I am...

Daily Affirmation

Acts of Kindness Towards Myself	Acts of Kindness Towards Others

Date:

Today I feel...

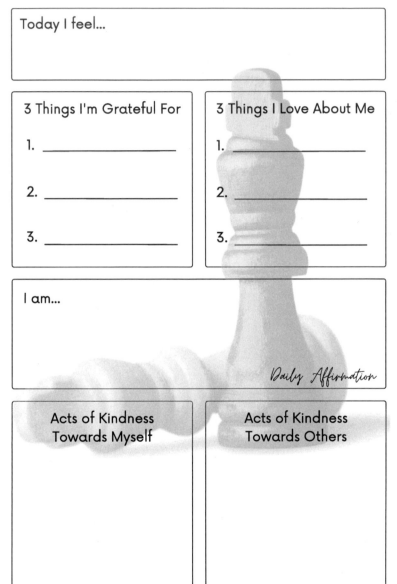

3 Things I'm Grateful For	3 Things I Love About Me
1. _____	1. _____
2. _____	2. _____
3. _____	3. _____

I am...

Daily Affirmation

Acts of Kindness Towards Myself	Acts of Kindness Towards Others

Date:

Today I feel...

3 Things I'm Grateful For	3 Things I Love About Me
1. _____	1. _____
2. _____	2. _____
3. _____	3. _____

I am...

Daily Affirmation

Acts of Kindness Towards Myself	Acts of Kindness Towards Others

Date:

Today I feel...

3 Things I'm Grateful For	3 Things I Love About Me
1. _____	1. _____
2. _____	2. _____
3. _____	3. _____

I am...

Daily Affirmation

Acts of Kindness Towards Myself	Acts of Kindness Towards Others

Date:

Today I feel...

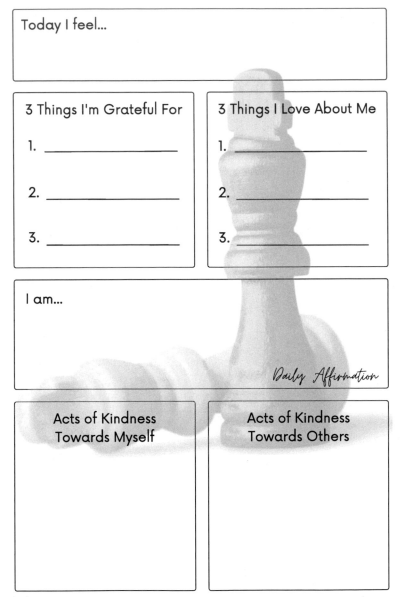

3 Things I'm Grateful For

1. _____

2. _____

3. _____

3 Things I Love About Me

1. _____

2. _____

3. _____

I am...

Daily Affirmation

Acts of Kindness
Towards Myself

Acts of Kindness
Towards Others

Date:

Today I feel...

3 Things I'm Grateful For	3 Things I Love About Me
1. _____	1. _____
2. _____	2. _____
3. _____	3. _____

I am...

Daily Affirmation

Acts of Kindness Towards Myself	Acts of Kindness Towards Others

Date:

Today I feel...

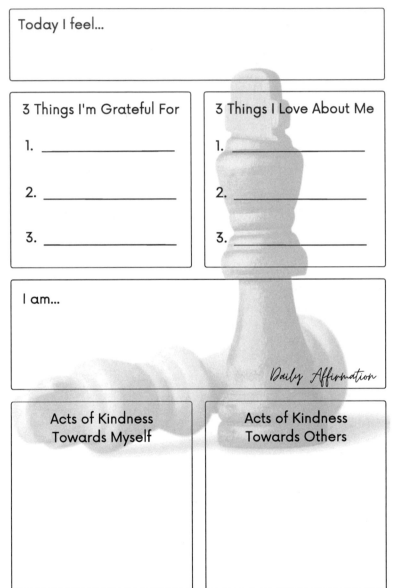

3 Things I'm Grateful For

1. _____

2. _____

3. _____

3 Things I Love About Me

1. _____

2. _____

3. _____

I am...

Daily Affirmation

Acts of Kindness
Towards Myself

Acts of Kindness
Towards Others

Date:

Today I feel...

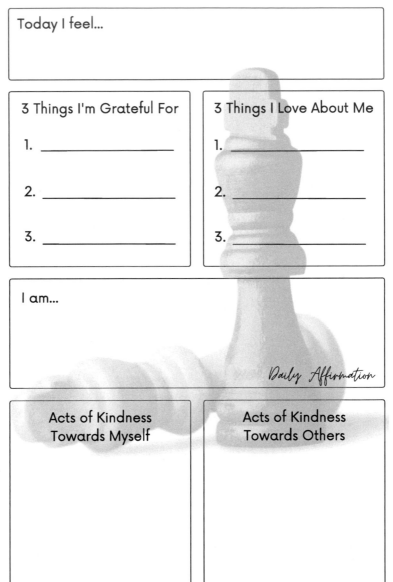

3 Things I'm Grateful For

1. _____

2. _____

3. _____

3 Things I Love About Me

1. _____

2. _____

3. _____

I am...

Daily Affirmation

Acts of Kindness
Towards Myself

Acts of Kindness
Towards Others

Date:

Today I feel...

3 Things I'm Grateful For

1. _____

2. _____

3. _____

3 Things I Love About Me

1. _____

2. _____

3. _____

I am...

Daily Affirmation

Acts of Kindness
Towards Myself

Acts of Kindness
Towards Others

Date:

Today I feel...

3 Things I'm Grateful For

1. _____

2. _____

3. _____

3 Things I Love About Me

1. _____

2. _____

3. _____

I am...

Daily Affirmation

Acts of Kindness
Towards Myself

Acts of Kindness
Towards Others

Date:

Today I feel...

3 Things I'm Grateful For

1. _____

2. _____

3. _____

3 Things I Love About Me

1. _____

2. _____

3. _____

I am...

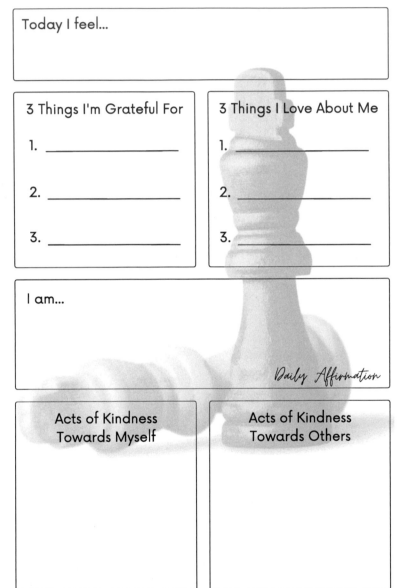

Daily Affirmation

Acts of Kindness
Towards Myself

Acts of Kindness
Towards Others

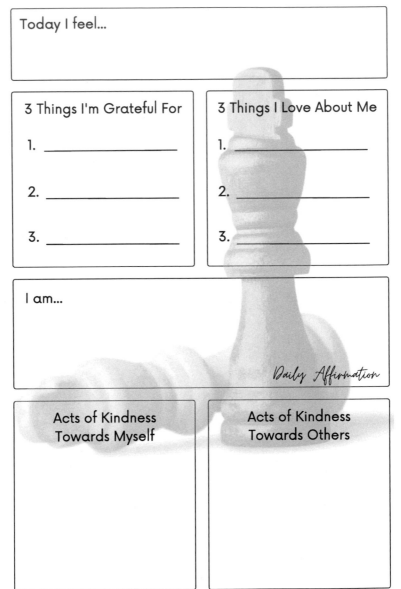

Date:

Today I feel...

3 Things I'm Grateful For

1. _____

2. _____

3. _____

3 Things I Love About Me

1. _____

2. _____

3. _____

I am...

Daily Affirmation

Acts of Kindness Towards Myself

Acts of Kindness Towards Others

Date:

Today I feel...

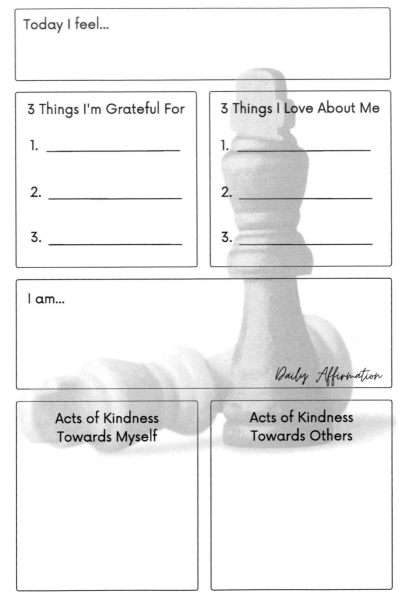

3 Things I'm Grateful For

1. _____

2. _____

3. _____

3 Things I Love About Me

1. _____

2. _____

3. _____

I am...

Daily Affirmation

Acts of Kindness
Towards Myself

Acts of Kindness
Towards Others

Date:

Today I feel...

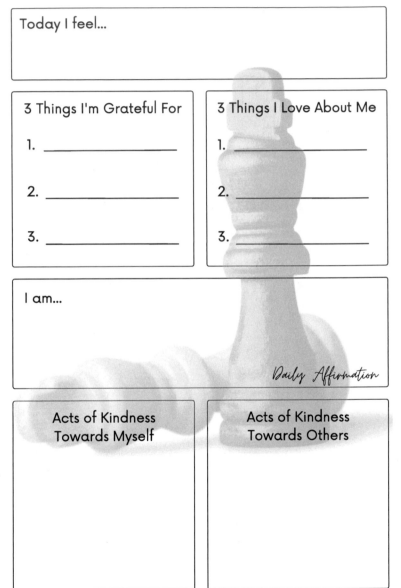

3 Things I'm Grateful For	3 Things I Love About Me
1. _____	1. _____
2. _____	2. _____
3. _____	3. _____

I am...

Daily Affirmation

Acts of Kindness Towards Myself	Acts of Kindness Towards Others

Date:

Today I feel...

3 Things I'm Grateful For

1. _____

2. _____

3. _____

3 Things I Love About Me

1. _____

2. _____

3. _____

I am...

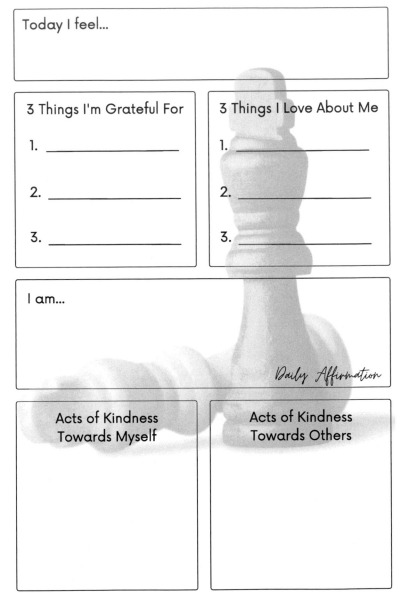

Daily Affirmation

Acts of Kindness
Towards Myself

Acts of Kindness
Towards Others

Date:

Today I feel...

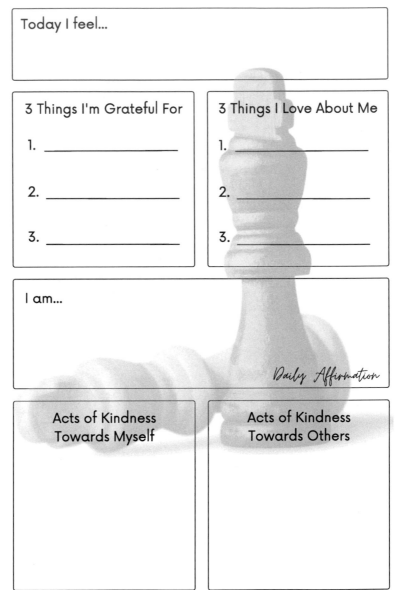

3 Things I'm Grateful For	3 Things I Love About Me
1. _____	1. _____
2. _____	2. _____
3. _____	3. _____

I am...

Daily Affirmation

Acts of Kindness Towards Myself	Acts of Kindness Towards Others

Date:

Today I feel...

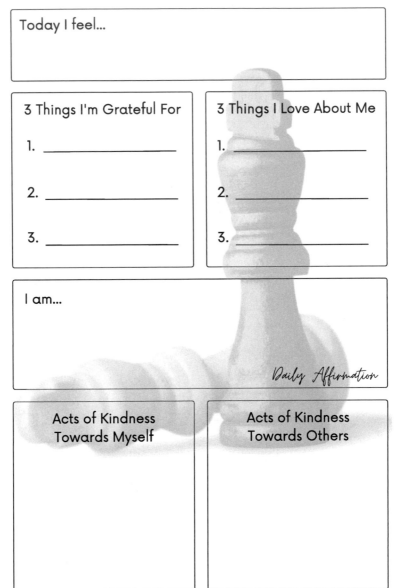

3 Things I'm Grateful For	3 Things I Love About Me
1. _____	1. _____
2. _____	2. _____
3. _____	3. _____

I am...

Daily Affirmation

Acts of Kindness Towards Myself	Acts of Kindness Towards Others

Date:

Today I feel...

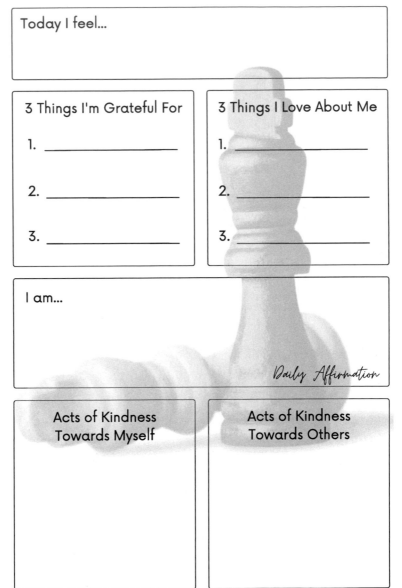

3 Things I'm Grateful For	3 Things I Love About Me
1. _____	1. _____
2. _____	2. _____
3. _____	3. _____

I am...

Daily Affirmation

Acts of Kindness
Towards Myself

Acts of Kindness
Towards Others

Date:

Today I feel...

3 Things I'm Grateful For

1. _____

2. _____

3. _____

3 Things I Love About Me

1. _____

2. _____

3. _____

I am...

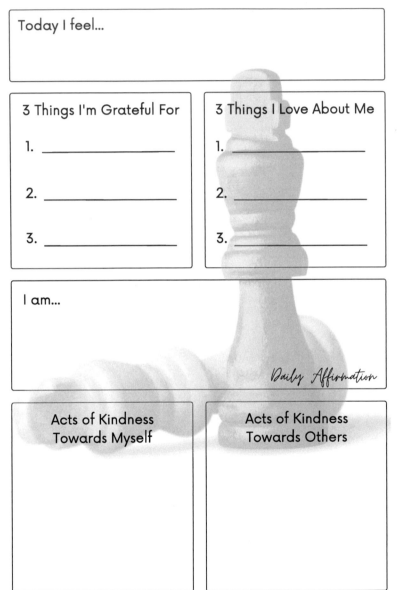

Daily Affirmation

Acts of Kindness
Towards Myself

Acts of Kindness
Towards Others

Date:

Today I feel...

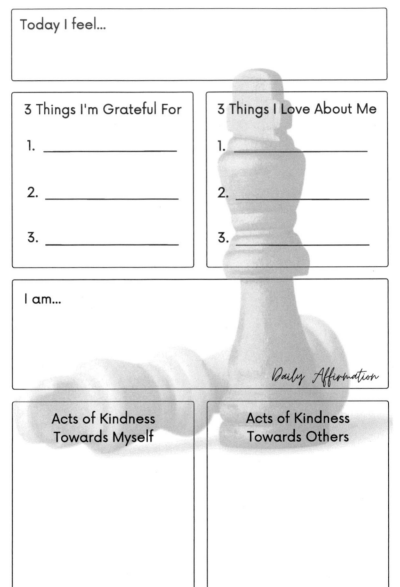

3 Things I'm Grateful For	3 Things I Love About Me
1. _____	1. _____
2. _____	2. _____
3. _____	3. _____

I am...

Daily Affirmation

Acts of Kindness Towards Myself	Acts of Kindness Towards Others

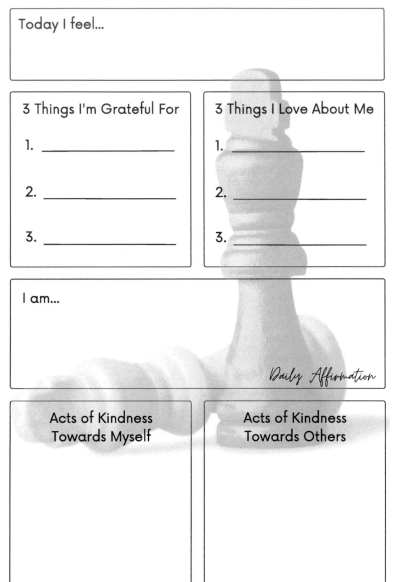

Date:

Today I feel...

3 Things I'm Grateful For	3 Things I Love About Me
1. _____	1. _____
2. _____	2. _____
3. _____	3. _____

I am...

Daily Affirmation

Acts of Kindness Towards Myself	Acts of Kindness Towards Others

Date:

Today I feel...

3 Things I'm Grateful For

1. _____

2. _____

3. _____

3 Things I Love About Me

1. _____

2. _____

3. _____

I am...

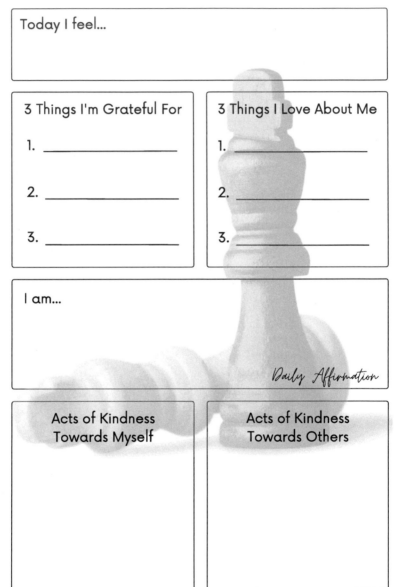

Daily Affirmation

Acts of Kindness
Towards Myself

Acts of Kindness
Towards Others

Date:

Today I feel...

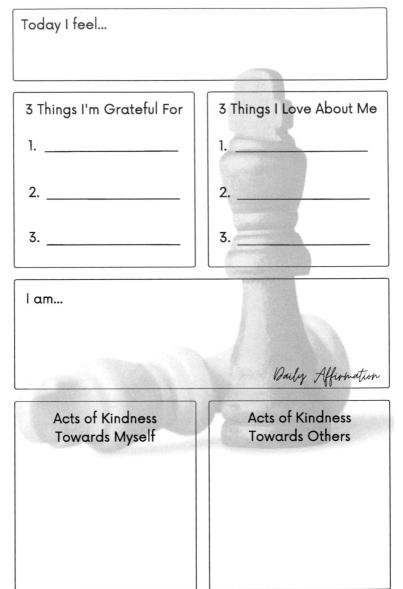

3 Things I'm Grateful For	3 Things I Love About Me
1. _____	1. _____
2. _____	2. _____
3. _____	3. _____

I am...

Daily Affirmation

Acts of Kindness Towards Myself	Acts of Kindness Towards Others

Date:

Today I feel...

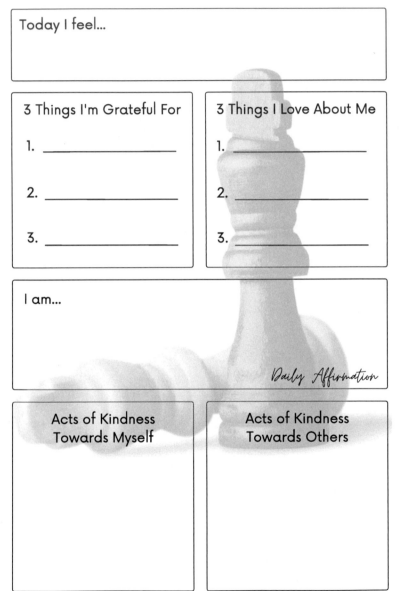

3 Things I'm Grateful For

1. _____

2. _____

3. _____

3 Things I Love About Me

1. _____

2. _____

3. _____

I am...

Daily Affirmation

Acts of Kindness
Towards Myself

Acts of Kindness
Towards Others

Date:

Today I feel...

3 Things I'm Grateful For

1. _____

2. _____

3. _____

3 Things I Love About Me

1. _____

2. _____

3. _____

I am...

Daily Affirmation

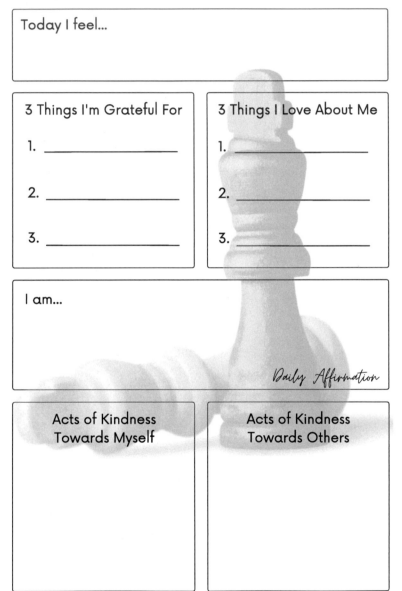

**Acts of Kindness
Towards Myself**

**Acts of Kindness
Towards Others**

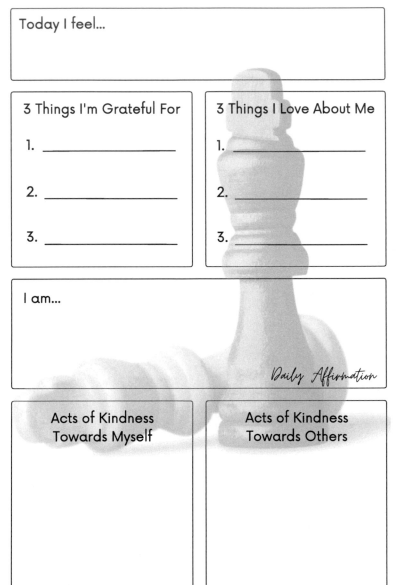

Date:

Today I feel...

3 Things I'm Grateful For

1. _____

2. _____

3. _____

3 Things I Love About Me

1. _____

2. _____

3. _____

I am...

Daily Affirmation

Acts of Kindness Towards Myself

Acts of Kindness Towards Others

Date:

Today I feel...

3 Things I'm Grateful For	3 Things I Love About Me
1. _____	1. _____
2. _____	2. _____
3. _____	3. _____

I am...

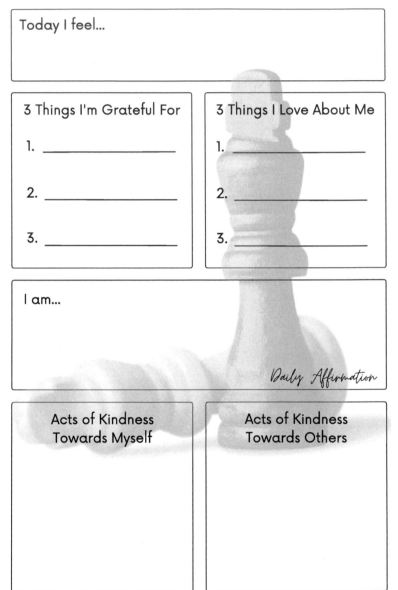

Daily Affirmation

Acts of Kindness Towards Myself	Acts of Kindness Towards Others

Date:

Today I feel...

3 Things I'm Grateful For

1. _____

2. _____

3. _____

3 Things I Love About Me

1. _____

2. _____

3. _____

I am...

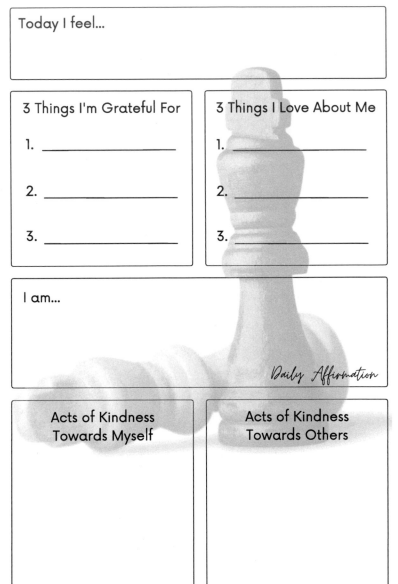

Daily Affirmation

Acts of Kindness
Towards Myself

Acts of Kindness
Towards Others

Date:

Today I feel...

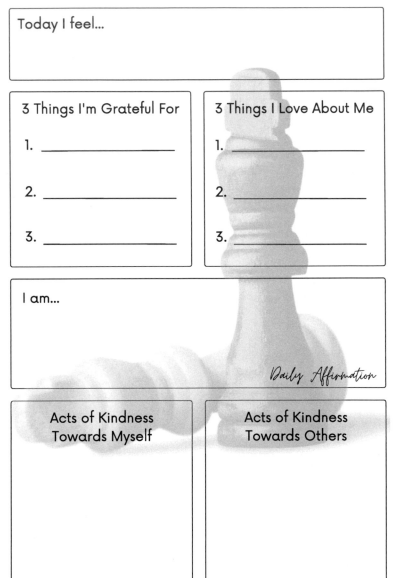

3 Things I'm Grateful For

1. _____

2. _____

3. _____

3 Things I Love About Me

1. _____

2. _____

3. _____

I am...

Daily Affirmation

Acts of Kindness Towards Myself

Acts of Kindness Towards Others

Date:

Today I feel...

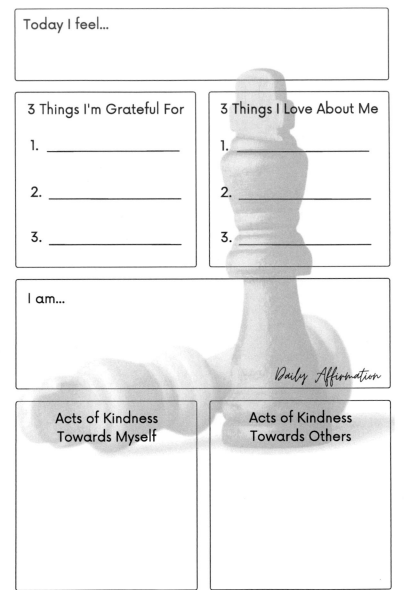

3 Things I'm Grateful For

1. _____

2. _____

3. _____

3 Things I Love About Me

1. _____

2. _____

3. _____

I am...

Daily Affirmation

Acts of Kindness
Towards Myself

Acts of Kindness
Towards Others

Date:

Today I feel...

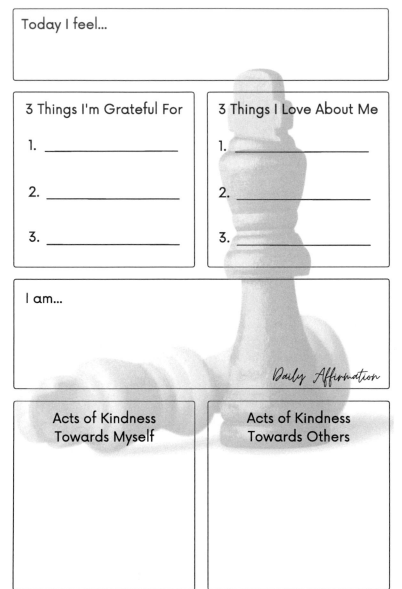

3 Things I'm Grateful For

1. _____

2. _____

3. _____

3 Things I Love About Me

1. _____

2. _____

3. _____

I am...

Daily Affirmation

Acts of Kindness
Towards Myself

Acts of Kindness
Towards Others

Date:

Today I feel...

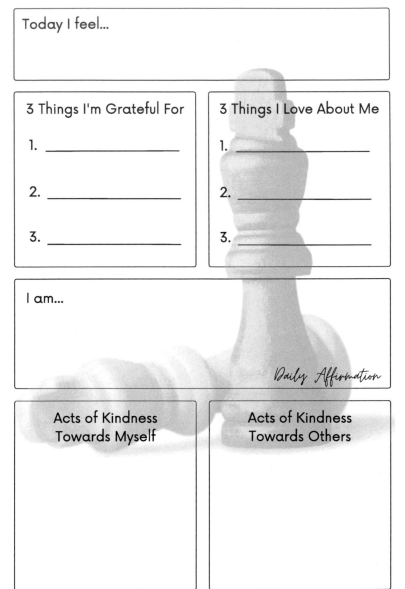

3 Things I'm Grateful For

1. _____

2. _____

3. _____

3 Things I Love About Me

1. _____

2. _____

3. _____

I am...

Daily Affirmation

Acts of Kindness
Towards Myself

Acts of Kindness
Towards Others

Hello King,

Congratulations for taking the necessary steps to become the best version of yourself. You deserve it!!

Sincerly,
Erika B

Made in the USA
Monee, IL
17 May 2022